D0284499

The Foreplay Gourmet

Over One Hundred
Outrageous Recipes
For Making Love

Other Books
Researched By
Chris Allen

1001 Sex Secrets Every Man Should Know
1001 Sex Secrets Every Woman Should Know
The Sex Secrets Tapes

The
Foreplay
Gourmet

Over One Hundred
Outrageous Recipes
For Making Love

Researched
by
Chris Allen

Copyright © 1995 by Chris Allen

All rights reserved. No portion of this book may be
reproduced in any form, or by any means, electronic or
mechanical, including photocopying, recording, or any
information storage retrieval system, without the written
permission of the publisher.

Published by
Creative Fire
Post Office Box 1122
Alcoa, TN 37701-1122

ISBN: 0-9636454-3-9

Printed in the United States of America

Contents

Preface   9

Appetizers For Him

Button Bite Delight   13
The Silk Snake Charmer   14
Brushing Bride   15
Lipquick   16
Name That Nipple   17
The Maraschino Knot   18
The Reflective Tease   18
The Stocking Buff   19
Rolling In The Valley   20

Appetizers For Her

Baby Elephant Trunks   23
The Follicle Frolic   24
The Cotton Spritzer   25
Featherotica   26
The Silky Way   27
The Dough Roll   28
Toe-tal Relaxation   29
Petal Piñata   30
The Glistening Forearm   31
Bath and Berries   32

Appetizers For Both

Vi-ssage   35
Fingerotica   36
Lip-o-suction   37
X-ellent Surprise   38
The Magic Mattress   39
Re-back-sation   40

Entrees For Him

The Pleasure Cone   43
The Beaded Mill   44
The Coconut Valley   45
Asti Spermanti   46
The Hot Diamond   47
The Tawdry Tortilla   48
The Phallic Fireball   49
The Peppermint Pleaser   50
Baskin Throbbins   51
Winter Wonderhands   52
The Passion Peach   53
The Licorice Lasso   54
Duck and Cover   55
Penis Butter & Jelly   56
Fruit Roll Frenzy   57
Ecstasy-clair   58
Priority Male   59
The Concord Catapult   60
The Sandshake   61
The Glazed Halo   62
The Fireman's Hose   63
The Dangling Apples   64
The Cardboard Collar   65
Granu-lattio   66

To Order Additional
Copies Of This Book
In The United States
Or Canada,
Call Toll-Free
1-800-444-PLAY

Please remember to exercise extreme caution
and common sense when attempting any of the
techniques described in this book. Neither the
author, publisher nor anyone associated with
the printing, promotion, sale or distribution of
this book are liable for any injuries or damage
to personal property resulting from actions
associated with the material presented within.
Use at your own risk.

	The Lounge Lizard	67
	The Pecan Mummy	68
	Schnapps and Rubbers	69
	Frankphoria	70
	The Tropical Shake	71
Entrees For Her	The Menthol Marinade	75
	Whipped Cream Dream	76
	Parad-ice	77
	The Grapes of Rapture	78
	Kiwi Supreme	79
	Penisicle	80
	Cotton Can-delight	81
	Bananirvana	82
	The Bunny Melt	83
	Showergasm	84
	Buzz Lips	85
	OrgasM&M	86
	The Venus Butterfly	87
	Sta-puffed Stimulation	88
	The Sensuous Summons	89
	Sue-Bliss	90
	Strawberry-lation	91
	The Tepid Triangle	92
	The Sultry Sucker	93
	Cake Dec-arousal	94
	Breath Massage	95
	Egg-stasy	96
	Canta-lucious	97
	Auto-erotica	98
	C-Delicious	99
	Jell-O-gasm	100
Entrees For Both	Notable Potable	103
	3-Minute 4-Play	104
	Confection Affection	105
	The Twinkling Twosome	106
	The Vineyard's Mist	107
	Carnal Coupons	108
	Chocolate Cherries Jubilee	109
	Erotic Roulette	110
	Nipple Shot	111
	Fore-Playback	112
	Pudding Pleasure	113
	Pasta Passion	114
	69 Card Pick-Up	115
Desserts	Country Coitus	119
	In-line Enchantment	120
	Patio-gasm	121
	Hy-stair-ia	122
	The Horizontal Tune-Up	123
	The Titillating Table	124
	Horn of Panty	125
	Waterbedlum	126
	Gotta Have Mower	127

To Order Additional
Copies Of This Book
In The United States
Or Canada,
Call Toll-Free
1-800-444-PLAY

IN CASE YOU MISSED IT THE FIRST TIME:

Please remember to exercise extreme caution
and common sense when attempting any of the
techniques described in this book. Neither the
author, publisher nor anyone associated with
the printing, promotion, sale or distribution of
this book are liable for any injuries or damage
to personal property resulting from actions
associated with the material presented within.
Use at your own risk.

Preface

If you don't have a sense of humor, GET ONE before you continue reading this book.

The sexual techniques described within are unusual, unique, some even downright bizarre. They were related to me over the past four years by everyday people who, like most of us, are constantly looking for new ways to keep the variety and passion in their relationships.

Before you dive into "the good stuff," there are probably a few things we should get straight. First, more than any earth-shattering physical technique, the most important thing you can give your partner in the bedroom is respect. Nothing does more to create a sense of trust, security and, ultimately, an environment where they feel comfortable enough to try new things. If there's something in this book that you want to try, but your partner doesn't, respect their wishes and let it go. Guilt trips will get you nowhere. Also, when your partner feels they've been treated with respect, they're much more likely to honor your request sometime in the future. Be patient and everybody wins.

Second, these recipes are meant to serve as guides. Use your imagination and come up with your own variations. There is no "right" or "wrong" way to do anything when it comes to matters of personal preference.

Finally, always remember to show your partner you love them in ways outside of the bedroom. While sex is best with someone you love, it should never become the only expression of your love. Showing love for your partner in non-sexual ways takes a great deal of the pressure off your sexual encounters and allows you both to relax, let down your guard and have FUN.

Which is exactly what this book is all about!

Appetizers
For Him

Button Bite Delight

1 man, topless
1 woman, clothing optional
1 old shirt, with buttons

1. Have man put on old shirt and button it completely.

2. Place topmost button between teeth and, holding shirt against man's chest, pull head back to remove.

3. If shirt has pocket, pull open with finger, open mouth and let button fall into pocket.

4. Open shirt and kiss newly exposed chest area.

5. Move on to next button and repeat steps 2 through 4.

6. Once bottom-most button has been bitten off, completely remove shirt.

   Note: Before starting, you may want to cut some of the threads holding each button for easy removal.

The Silk Snake Charmer

1 man, naked
1 woman, clothing optional
1 silk scarf

1. Have man lie on his back.

2. Hold silk scarf by one end and gently run loose end along his entire body.

3. Delicately tease genitals by gliding scarf back and forth across penis.

4. When penis becomes erect, hold scarf above it and gently wrap around shaft and head. Slowly pull up, allowing scarf to unwind.

5. Wrap scarf loosely around your hand. With other hand, press penis against or near man's stomach.

6. Gently stroke testicles and inner thighs with scarf.

7. With scarf still wrapped loosely around hand, again glide over entire body.

Brushing Bride

1 man, naked
1 woman, naked

1. Have man lie on his stomach.

2. On hands and knees, bending over foot, position his ankle between your breasts.

3. Gently rub breasts up leg to calf, then back down.

4. Gradually move all the way up leg until you reach buttocks.

5. Delicately glide nipples over buttocks, then slowly work your way down the other leg.

6. Have man turn over on his back.

7. Straddle leg, rubbing breasts back and forth up leg until you reach genitals.

8. Use hand to press penis against man's stomach and, using other hand to hold breast, gently rub against testicles.

Lipquick

1 man, clothed
1 woman, clothed
1 tube lipstick, any color

1. With man standing, kneel in front of him.

2. Unzip pants and take out penis.

3. Hold penis by shaft and rub a generous amount of lipstick on head.

4. Use head of penis to apply lipstick to lips.

5. Put penis back into pants and zip up.

Note: This technique is generally used before going out for the evening.

Name That Nipple

1 man, clothing optional
1 woman, topless
1 bag hard candy, assorted flavors
1 blindfold
1 washcloth, damp

1. Have man sit in a chair, blindfolded.

2. Place hard candy in your mouth until it begins to dissolve.

3. Take out candy and rub generously on and around nipple.

4. Invite man to gently suck nipple and guess the candy's flavor. Establish a number you will play to (for example: five correct guesses, he wins; five incorrect, you win) as well as a prize for the winner.

5. Repeat steps 2 through 4 using different flavor hard candy and other nipple.

6. Use washcloth to remove previous flavor from nipple and continue until number is reached.

The Maraschino Knot

1 man, clothing optional
1 woman, topless
2 maraschino cherries, with stems

1. Pinch nipples so they become erect.

2. Tie maraschino cherry stems around each nipple.

3. Have man gently lick, suck and bite cherries.

The Reflective Tease

1 man, naked
1 woman, clothing optional
1 tube lipstick, red

1. Wait for man to get into shower.

2. Sneak into bathroom with lipstick.

3. Write a sensuous message on mirror. Examples: "I'm waiting for you," "Meet me in the bedroom," "Let me dry you with my tongue," etc.

The Stocking Buff

1 man, naked
1 woman, clothing optional
1 silk stocking

1. Have man stand, legs slightly apart.

2. Kneel, facing man's right side.

3. Take silk stocking and gently place between legs at calf level. Hold stocking at both ends.

4. Slowly run stocking back and forth over right calf, gradually working upwards to inner thigh.

5. Move behind man and run stocking back and forth down front of leg.

6. Move to other side of man and repeat steps 3 and 4 with left leg.

7. Lift arms up so stocking touches testicles. Alternate arms up and down, delicately caressing testicles with stocking.

Rolling In The Valley

1 man, naked
1 woman, topless
1 condom

1. Have man lie on his back.

2. Caress and gently stroke inner thighs, penis and testicles until penis becomes erect.

3. Unwrap condom and place on head of erect penis.

4. Straddle man's legs and place penis between breasts.

5. Use hands to push breasts together and, in a downward motion, unroll condom onto shaft of penis.

Appetizers
For Her

Baby Elephant Trunks

1 woman, naked
1 man, clothing optional

1. Have woman lie on her back, knees slightly bent, legs apart.

2. Extend right hand with palm down. Bend wrist so fingers are pointing down.

3. Gently place back of hand, at wrist, against bottom portion of vagina.

4. With smooth strokes, glide entire hand, including fingers, up and over vagina.

5. As hand rises above vagina, gently brush fingertips against pubic hair.

6. Immediately repeat steps 2 through 5 with left hand.

7. Alternate hands in continuous motion.

The Follicle Frolic

1 woman, clothing optional
1 man, clothing optional
1 hairbrush

1. Spread fingers and work through woman's hair until you reach scalp.

2. Use fingertips to vigorously massage scalp, moving from front of head to back.

3. Sit or stand behind woman, her head at same height as your chest.

4. Brush hair from front of scalp to back.

5. Have woman tilt head down. Brush from back of scalp to front.

6. Finish by again brushing hair from front to back.

The Cotton Spritzer

1 woman, with cotton panties
1 man, clothing optional
1 bottle wine

1. Have woman stand.

2. Kneel in front of her.

3. Pull panties open and pour a small amount of wine into crotch. Release.

4. Place open mouth against crotch of panties. Apply gentle suction to bring wine from panties into mouth.

5. Repeat steps 3 and 4.

Featherotica

1 woman, naked
1 man, clothing optional
1 feather duster

1. Have woman lie on her stomach.

2. Gently glide feather duster over calves, backs of knees, buttocks, back and neck.

3. Have woman turn over on her back.

4. Continue running feather duster over face, neck, breasts, thighs, arms and feet.

5. Place feather duster between legs and delicately brush vagina, clitoris, pubic hair and stomach.

6. Repeat step 5 several times.

The Silky Way

1 woman, naked
1 man, clothing optional
1 silk scarf

1. Have woman lie on her back.

2. Hold silk scarf at one end and gently run loose end across her entire body.

3. Elevate scarf so end barely touches nipple. Flick scarf up and down so it dances around nipple and breast.

4. Repeat with other breast.

5. Wrap scarf loosely around hand.

6. Gently run scarf along inner thighs.

7. Glide scarf over vagina, using back of hand on the upstroke, palm when caressing downward.

8. Finish by running hand, scarf still loosely wrapped around it, over woman's entire body.

The Dough Roll

1 woman, naked
1 man, clothing optional
1 rolling pin

1.   Have woman lie on her stomach.

2.   Take rolling pin and, starting at calves, roll back and forth, being careful not press too hard.

3.   Work your way up both legs, eventually moving to buttocks.

4.   Use rolling pin on left side of back, then right side.

5.   Finish by rolling from calf to shoulder on one side, then the other.

Toe-tal Relaxation

1 woman, clothing optional
1 man, clothing optional

1. Have woman lie on her back.

2. Grasp toes of one foot in palm and squeeze together.

3. Push toes back toward knee and, with other hand, run meat of thumb along arch of foot, from heel to toes.

4. Using thumb and first finger, pinch outside edge of foot, from heel to little toe.

5. With first and second finger, apply pressure to bottom of foot, just below toes, working from side to side.

6. Holding foot at ankle, elevate leg slightly. Grasp foot with other hand and gently rotate twenty times clockwise, then twenty times counterclockwise.

7. Repeat steps 1 through 6 with other foot.

Petal Piñata

1 woman, clothed
1 man, clothed
5 dozen flower petals

1. Out of woman's view, place flower petals in the crotch of your underwear.

2. With woman standing, slowly undress her.

3. Have woman, naked, lie face up on bed.

4. Stand on bed, straddling woman, and begin to undress.

5. As you remove underwear, flower petals will fall onto woman and bed, providing a sensual service on which to make love.

The Glistening Forearm

1 woman, naked
1 man, clothing optional
1 bottle baby oil

1. Have woman position herself on all fours, legs slightly apart.

2. Hold your arm out with palm facing up.

3. Apply baby oil to inside of forearm, from wrist to inner elbow.

4. Sit behind woman. Reach between legs and gently place inner elbow against vagina.

5. Pull arm back so it glides across vagina and clitoris. Wrist should now be touching vagina.

6. Push arm forward until inner elbow is again resting against vagina.

7. Repeat steps 5 and 6, varying speed and intensity.

Bath and Berries

1 woman, clothed
1 man, clothing optional
5 scented candles
1 glass wine

1. Before woman arrives home, draw a hot bath.

2. Place candles along edge of tub and light. Turn out all other lights.

3. When woman arrives, slowly undress her and escort to tub.

4. Have woman relax in tub as you bring her glass of wine.

5. Wash woman's back.

6. Leave woman alone in tub for approximately 20 to 30 minutes.

Note: You may also add bath beads, oils, etc.

Appetizers
For Both

Vi-ssage

1 man, clothing optional
1 woman, clothing optional

1. Slowly kiss and lick eyelids.

2. Place first and second finger of each hand on forehead just above eyebrows. Rub in circular motion.

3. Use same fingers to massage temples.

4. Continue using first and second fingers in a circular motion to relax jaw area, just in front of ear.

5. Softly lick around edge of ears. Nibble and apply gentle suction to ear lobes.

6. Finish with delicate kisses along the hairline behind ears and on back of neck.

Fingerotica

1. woman, clothing optional
1 man, clothing optional

1. Hold hand at palm and slowly insert tip of finger into mouth. Apply gentle suction.

2. Open mouth and slide finger farther in, up to second knuckle. Again, apply gentle suction.

3. Push entire finger into mouth and apply gentle suction. Run tip of tongue up, down and around finger.

4. Repeat steps 1 through 3 on remaining fingers.

Lip-o-suction

1 man, clothing optional
1 woman, clothing optional

1. Have partner lie face up on bed, eyes closed. Instruct partner that lips and mouth are to remain perfectly still.

2. As lightly as you can, touch partner's lower lip with the tip of your tongue.

3. Run tongue from one end of lower lip to the other and back.

4. Repeat steps 2 and 3 with upper lip.

5. Go back to lower lip and, this time, apply more pressure.

6. Do the same with upper lip.

7. Gently suck lower lip into your mouth and run tongue over it with quick, up-and-down flicks.

8. Stick tongue between lips and curl upward so tip is against back of upper lip. Glide from side to side.

9. Finish with slow, passionate, full-on kiss.

X-ellent Surprise

1 woman
1 man
1 pizza
1 bottle wine
1 X-rated videotape

1. On your way home for the evening and without your partner's knowledge, go by grocery store and buy a bottle of wine.

2. Stop by a restaurant and pick up a pizza for two.

3. Rent an adult tape from your local video store.

4. Head home and surprise partner.

The Magic Mattress

1 man
1 woman
1 stereo
2 stereo speakers

1. Before making love, lay stereo speakers flat, cones facing upward.

2. Slide each speaker underneath bed, one at head, one at foot, making sure speaker cable is of sufficient length as not to pose a danger of tripping.

3. Adjust bass of stereo to slightly higher-than-normal position.

4. Select music with rhythmic, pounding bass and let speakers vibrate bed in time with music.

Re-back-sation

1 woman, naked
1 man, naked
1 glass cinnamon schnapps
1 eyedropper

1. Have partner lie on stomach.

2. Fill eyedropper with schnapps.

3. Starting at tailbone, apply drops of schnapps along spine. Continue all the way up to hairline on neck, pausing to refill eyedropper as needed.

4. Go back to tailbone and use mouth and tip of tongue to delicately kiss and lick schnapps from partner's spine.

5. Switch places and repeat steps 1 through 4.

Entrees
For Him

The Pleasure Cone

1 man, naked
1 woman, clothed
1 ice cream cone
1 can whipped cream

1. Have man lie on his back.

2. Kiss, lick and apply gentle suction to penis, thighs and testicles until penis becomes erect.

3. Take ice cream cone and bite or cut off bottom, allowing only enough room for penis to fit though.

4. Insert penis through bottom of cone.

5. Fill open space between penis and cone with whipped cream. Liberally apply whipped cream to portion of penis protruding above cone.

6. Delicately lick whipped cream from penis. Nibble on cone in circular fashion, gradually performing fellatio.

7. Continue until orgasm or desired consistency of arousal.

The Beaded Mill

1 man, naked
1 woman, clothing optional
1 pearl necklace, long

1. Have man lie on his back.

2. Kiss, lick and apply gentle suction to penis, thighs and testicles until penis becomes erect.

3. Slowly wrap pearl necklace around penis, starting at bottom and working your way to top.

4. With palms and fingers straight, place penis between hands. Rub hands back and forth, as if trying to warm them.

5. Wrap one hand around penis and move pearls up and down along shaft.

6. Alternate between back-and-forth and up-and-down motion.

7. Repeat steps 4 through 6 until orgasm or desired consistency of arousal.

    Note: You may substitute any beaded necklace for the pearls.

The Coconut Valley

1 man, naked
1 woman, naked
1 bottle coconut oil

1. Lie face up on bed.

2. Liberally apply coconut oil to breasts, concentrating on cleavage area.

3. Hold breasts together with hands, allowing only enough room for man to insert penis.

4. Have man straddle your waist and gently place penis between breasts.

5. Using hips, man moves penis in and out of cleavage area.

6. Repeat step 5, applying more oil if necessary, until orgasm or desired consistency of arousal.

    Note: You may substitute any fragrant lotion for coconut oil.

Asti Spermanti

1 man, naked
1 woman, clothing optional
1 glass champagne

1. Have man stand or lie on his back.

2. Sip champagne from glass. Do not swallow.

3. With champagne in mouth, apply lips to head of penis.

4. Open mouth slightly, being careful not to allow champagne to spill from mouth.

5. Quickly take penis into mouth.

6. Perform fellatio, pausing frequently to swish champagne around in mouth (bubbles should arise as a result of this action).

7. Continue step 6 until orgasm or desired consistency of arousal.

The Hot Diamond

1 man, naked
1 woman, clothing optional
1 washcloth

1. Have man lie on his back.

2. Place washcloth in sink and run hot water over it until completely saturated. Ring out washcloth, being careful not to scald hands.

3. Fold washcloth into quarters. Place in your hand so that it takes on a diamond shape (one corner on middle finger, one corner touching wrist, other corners on each side of hand).

4. Using free hand, hold man's penis near or against his stomach. Gently place washcloth against man's testicles, being careful not to press too hard at first.

5. Stimulate man's penis manually, while gradually increasing pressure of washcloth against testicles.

6. If washcloth begins to cool, repeat step 2.

7. Continue steps 5 and 6 until orgasm or desired consistency of arousal.

The Tawdry Tortilla

1 man, naked
1 woman, clothing optional
1 soft tortilla, flour or corn
1 tablespoon refried beans

1. Spread one tablespoon refried beans, room temperature, onto soft tortilla.

2. Have man stand or lie on his back.

3. Starting with underside, wrap tortilla tightly around penis.

4. Place your thumb and first finger around tortilla at base of penis to keep firmly in place.

5. Slowly begin to nibble around edge of tortilla protruding beyond head of penis.

6. Nibble tortilla all the way down shaft of penis, pausing frequently to perform fellatio.

7. Continue step 6 until orgasm or desired consistency of arousal.

The Phallic Fireball

.1 man, naked
1 woman, clothing optional
1 bottle hot sauce, small

1. Have man lie on his back.

2. Kiss, lick and apply gentle suction to penis, thighs and testicles until penis becomes erect.

3. Hold bottle of hot sauce approximately 4 inches above penis. Tilt bottle until a single drop falls directly onto opening at tip of penis.

4. For added stimulation, gently blow on tip of penis.

5. Perform fellatio until orgasm or desired consistency of arousal.

    Note: After performing this technique, you may want to wash penis with damp cloth before allowing it to enter vagina.

The Peppermint Pleaser

1 man, naked
1 woman, clothing optional
1 peppermint

1. Have man lie on his back.

2. Unwrap peppermint and place in your mouth.

3. After peppermint starts to dissolve, begin to perform fellatio.

4. After penis is sufficiently erect, use tongue to place peppermint directly on tip of penis.

5. Gently blow on penis for added stimulation.

6. Take peppermint back into mouth and resume fellatio until orgasm or desired consistency of arousal.

Baskin Throbbins

1 man, naked
1 woman, clothing optional
1 scoop ice cream, any flavor

1. Have man lie on his back.

2. Place a generous portion of ice cream in your mouth.

3. Purse lips and use tongue to push ice cream to front of mouth.

4. Barely touch head of man's penis with ice cream, slowly tracing rings around it.

5. As ice cream begins to melt, gradually accept more of man's penis into mouth.

6. Perform fellatio, making sure to lick any drops of melted ice cream that have run down penis onto testicles.

7. Continue until orgasm or desired consistency of arousal.

> Note: It is best to use ice cream that is smooth, without any chunks of fruit, cookies, candy bars, etc.

Winter Wonderhands

1 man, naked
1 woman, clothing optional
1 towel
2 handfuls snow

1. Fold towel in half.

2. Have man lie on his back with buttocks and back of thighs resting on towel.

3. Kiss, lick and apply gentle suction to penis, thighs and testicles until penis becomes erect.

4. Step outside and collect two handfuls of clean snow.

5. With man still on his back, pack both handfuls of snow around the shaft of his penis, leaving only the head exposed.

6. Apply gentle suction to head of penis, tracing circles around it with your tongue.

7. As melted snow trickles down inner thighs and testicles, perform fellatio on exposed area of penis.

8. Continue until orgasm or desired consistency of arousal.

The Passion Peach

1 man, naked
1 woman, clothing optional
1 peach, large

1. From top of peach, cut a circle all the way through and remove, including pit.

2. With man standing, kiss, lick and apply gentle suction to penis, thighs and testicles until penis becomes erect.

3. Slide penis through hole in peach.

4. Perform fellatio while rotating peach around shaft of penis.

5. Gently squeeze peach, licking juice as it comes out.

6. Continue steps 4 and 5 until orgasm or desired consistency of arousal.

The Licorice Lasso

1 man, naked
1 woman, naked
1 bag licorice whips

1. Have man lie on bed, arms above head.

2. Take one strand of licorice and tie his right wrist to bed post.

3. Now take another strand of licorice and tie left wrist to corresponding bed post.

4. Kiss, lick, stroke and generally tease man over the majority of his body.

5. When penis is erect, tie another strand of licorice around it.

6. Perform fellatio, pulling on licorice whip to guide penis into mouth.

7. Continue until orgasm or desired consistency of arousal.

Duck and Cover

1 man, naked
1 woman, clothing optional
1 packet duck sauce

1. Have man lie on his back.

2. Heat packet of duck sauce in microwave for approximately 8 seconds at full power (do not attempt if sauce is in foil packet).

3. Tear open corner of packet and hold 4 to 6 inches above penis.

4. Gently squeeze packet so a thin stream of duck sauce runs onto penis, testicles and inner thighs.

5. When packet is empty, slowly lick duck sauce from inner thighs, then testicles.

6. Perform fellatio, using tongue to remove remainder of duck sauce from penis.

7. Continue until orgasm or desired consistency of arousal.

Note: You may substitute sweet and sour for duck sauce.

Penis Butter & Jelly

1 man, naked
1 woman, clothing optional
1 jar peanut butter, smooth
1 jar jelly, any flavor

1. Have man lie on his back.

2. Caress and gently stroke penis, testicles and thighs until penis becomes erect.

3. Dip finger into jar of peanut butter and scoop out approximately one teaspoon.

4. Use finger to apply peanut butter to penis, spreading evenly around head and shaft.

5. Use same finger to scoop approximately one teaspoon of jelly from jar.

6. Place jelly in your mouth. Do not swallow.

7. Perform fellatio, mixing peanut butter and jelly together.

8. Continue until orgasm or desired consistency of arousal.

Fruit Roll Frenzy

1 man, naked
1 woman, clothing optional
1 pressed fruit roll, any flavor

1. Have man lie on his back.

2. Kiss, lick and apply gentle suction to penis, thighs and testicles until penis becomes erect.

3. Wrap fruit roll firmly around penis. Lick end of fruit roll and press against other end to secure.

4. Perform fellatio.

5. Continue until orgasm or desired consistency of arousal.

Ecstasy-clair

1 man, naked
1 woman, clothing optional
1 chocolate eclair

1. Have man lie on his back.

2. Caress and gently stroke penis, thighs and testicles until penis becomes erect.

3. Using tongue and finger, remove filling from center of chocolate eclair.

4. Place hollow eclair over penis.

5. Slowly eat small portions of eclair off penis, performing fellatio as areas become exposed.

6. Continue until orgasm or desired consistency of arousal.

Priority Male

1 man, naked
1 woman, clothing optional
4 postage stamps, connected
1 stopwatch

1. Give man postage stamps and stopwatch.

2. Instruct man to go into bedroom and affix postage stamps in a ring around middle of flaccid penis. This is achieved by moistening one end stamp and overlapping onto the top of other end stamp. Stamps should not be stuck to the skin.

3. When completed, have him call you into bedroom and turn on stopwatch.

4. Using whatever visual, tactile or aural means imaginable, arouse man until penis becomes erect and breaks ring of stamps.

5. When stamps break, turn off stopwatch and note time.

6. Repeat steps 1 through 5 on random occasions, attempting to beat previous record.

The Concord Catapult

1 man, naked
1 woman, clothing optional
1 bunch grapes, seedless

1. Have man lie on his back, legs slightly apart, knees bent.

2. Caress and gently stroke penis, thighs and testicles until penis becomes erect.

3. Position mouth between man's knees.

4. Have man pick grape from bunch and, using first finger, hold it against underside of penis head.

5. Have man pull erect penis back toward stomach and release, propelling grape toward your mouth.

6. When a predetermined number of grapes have been successfully caught, or when erection begins to subside, perform fellatio with grape(s) in mouth.

7. Continue until orgasm or desired consistency of arousal.

The Sandshake

1 man, naked
1 woman, clothing optional
1 beach, sandy
1 cup water
1 bottle suntan lotion

1. Have man dig hole in sand deep enough to be buried in.

2. Have man lie face up in hole.

3. Cover man's body with sand, leaving portion of head exposed for breathing. Pack sand firmly so movement is restricted.

4. Locate portion of sand covering penis. Remove only enough sand to expose penis.

5. Pour water over penis to remove extraneous grains of sand.

6. Apply suntan lotion liberally over hand.

7. Stimulate penis manually.

8. Continue until orgasm or desired consistency of arousal.

The Glazed Halo

1 man, naked
1 woman, clothing optional
1 glazed doughnut

1. Have man lie on his back.

2. Caress and gently stroke penis, thighs and testicles until penis becomes erect.

3. Place glazed doughnut over penis.

4. Nibble around edges of glazed doughnut, pausing frequently to flick tongue around head and shaft of penis.

5. When doughnut is gone, begin performing fellatio.

6. Continue until orgasm or desired consistency of arousal.

The Fireman's Hose

1 man, naked
1 woman, clothing optional
1 bottle hand lotion

1. Have man lie on his back, legs slightly apart, knees bent.

2. Sit cross-legged between man's legs.

3. Apply lotion liberally to palms. Rub hands together, warming lotion.

4. With left hand, grasp penis at base of shaft. Pull hand towards you until it clears head of penis.

5. As soon as left hand leaves base of shaft, grasp with right hand. Pull hand toward you, grasping base with left hand again, and so on.

6. For additional stimulation, vary rate hands move over penis and amount of pressure applied.

7. Continue until orgasm or desired consistency of arousal.

Note: Wipe hand lotion from penis before attempting intercourse.

The Dangling Apples

1 man, naked
1 woman, clothing optional
2 spiced crab apples
1 piece thread, 4 to 5 inches long

1. Tie crab apples to each end of thread.

2. With man standing, caress and gently stroke penis, testicles and thighs until penis becomes erect.

3. Place thread over base of penis. Crab apples should hang next to testicles.

4. Alternate between licking, lightly nibbling and applying gentle suction to crab apples and testicles.

5. Perform fellatio, pausing frequently to bite off small portion of crab apples.

6. Continue until orgasm or desired consistency of arousal.

The Cardboard Collar

1 man, naked
1 woman, clothing optional
1 toilet paper core

1. Have man sit.

2. Tear off 1/3 to 1/2 of toilet paper core and discard.

3. Place remaining portion of toilet paper core over flaccid penis shaft, head of penis protruding from end.

4. Caress testicles while kissing, licking and applying gentle suction to head of penis. As penis becomes erect, toilet paper core will constrict shaft of penis, making head much more sensitive.

5. Continue teasing testicles and penis head with tongue, mouth and hands for approximately 5 minutes.

6. Use fingers to tear toilet paper core off penis. Now shaft will be extra-sensitive.

7. Perform fellatio

8. Continue until orgasm or desired consistency of arousal.

Granu-lattio

1 **man, naked**
1 **woman, clothing optional**
1 **box brown sugar, granulated**
1 **saucer**

1. Have man lie on his back.

2. Pour brown sugar into saucer.

3. Use tongue to moisten underside of penis shaft and head.

4. Press penis into brown sugar.

5. Place mouth over penis and close. Keeping lips and mouth still, gently move tongue back and forth, dissolving brown sugar.

6. When brown sugar has completely dissolved, perform fellatio.

7. Continue until orgasm or desired consistency of arousal.

The Lounge Lizard

1 man, naked
1 woman, clothing optional
1 lounge chair, webbed
2 pillows
1 roll masking tape

1. Adjust back of lounge chair so it is completely flat.

2. Place pillows, lengthwise, directly underneath lounge chair.

3. Pull center-most webbing apart and tape to other straps, creating an opening in center of chair at least 5 inches wide.

4. Have man lie face down in lounge chair, his penis hanging through opening.

5. Position yourself under lounge chair and perform fellatio.

6. Continue until orgasm or desired consistency of arousal.

Note: This technique can also be performed using a hammock in place of lounge chair.

The Pecan Mummy

1 man, naked
1 woman, clothing optional
1 pecan twirl pastry

1. Have man stand.

2. Take pecan twirl, peel outer circle and break off. Remaining portion of pastry should be sufficiently moist and will not break.

3. Kneeling in front of man, peel end of remaining portion and place at base of penis.

4. Unroll pecan twirl, wrapping around penis, moving up shaft with each revolution.

5. When penis is completely wrapped in pecan twirl, delicately nibble on it, pausing frequently to lick and apply gentle suction to penis head.

6. When pecan twirl is gone, perform fellatio.

7. Continue until orgasm or desired consistency of arousal.

Schnapps and Rubbers

1 man, naked
1 woman, clothing optional
1 condom, unlubricated
1 bottle peppermint schnapps
1 rubber band

1. Unroll condom half way and fill 2/3 with schnapps.

2. Have man sit in chair. Push on base of penis so it is pointing downward. Bring condom to head of penis. Unroll remaining half over penis. Place rubber band over penis next to condom ring, reinforcing seal.

3. Carefully work condom upwards onto penis until snug. Place hands, one next to the other, around condom, completely covering penis.

4. Alternate hands, squeezing and releasing, sending schnapps rushing from top of condom to bottom.

5. Bite tiny hole in condom reservoir. Position your head 8 to 10 inches away. Have man squeeze schnapps into mouth.

6. Remove condom and perform fellatio.

7. Continue until orgasm or desired consistency of arousal.

Frankphoria

1 **man, naked**
1 **woman, clothing optional**
1 **hot dog bun**
1 **bottle ketchup**
1 **bottle mustard**

1. Have man stand.

2. Caress and gently stroke penis, testicles and thighs until penis becomes erect.

3. Open hot dog bun and place penis inside.

4. Apply ketchup and mustard to shaft.

5. Gently nibble bun away from penis, pausing frequently to lick condiments with tongue.

6. When bun has been consumed, perform fellatio.

7. Continue until orgasm or desired consistency of arousal.

The Tropical Shake

1 man, naked
1 woman, clothing optional
1 banana

1. Use knife to cut slit in banana peel lengthwise, being careful not to cut completely in half.

2. Pull cut ends apart and carefully remove banana peel.

3. Have man lie on his back.

4. Caress and gently stroke penis, testicles and thighs until penis becomes erect.

5. Wrap banana peel around penis.

6. Grasp peel with hand and manually stimulate penis with deliberate up-and-down motion.

7. Continue until orgasm or desired consistency of arousal.

Entrees
For Her

The Menthol Marinade

1 woman, naked
1 man, clothing optional
1 mentholated cough drop, any flavor

1. Unwrap menthol cough drop and place it in your mouth.

2. Kiss woman's legs, inner thighs and stomach, giving the cough drop time to partially dissolve.

3. Begin to perform cunnilingus.

4. Along with your usual oral sex techniques, rub the tip of your tongue on cough drop and trace circles around the clitoris.

5. For additional stimulation, pause periodically and gently blow on clitoris. Resume cunnilingus.

6. Repeat steps 4 and 5 until orgasm or desired consistency of arousal.

Whipped Cream Dream

1 woman, naked
1 man, clothing optional
1 can whipped cream

1. Have woman lie on her back.

2. Apply whipped cream liberally over woman's entire body. Pay special attention to nipples, navel and bikini line.

3. Slowly and delicately lick whipped cream off woman's body. Deliberate flicks of the tongue are generally more stimulating than a flat-tongued motion. In some cases, you may alternate.

4. Leave whipped cream on tongue and begin to perform cunnilingus.

5. Continue until orgasm or desired consistency of arousal.

Note: Always use whipped cream canned under pressure. Non-dairy whipped topping from a bowl will provide less-than-satisfactory results.

Parad-ice

1 woman, naked
1 man, clothing optional
1 ice cube

1. Have woman sit or lie on her back.

2. Place ice cube in your mouth.

3. Open mouth slightly and use tongue to push ice cube to front of mouth, only a small portion protruding beyond lips.

4. Slowly glide ice cube over woman's neck, breasts, stomach, thighs and legs.

5. Place mouth approximately 6 inches above nipples. Let drops of melted ice fall until nipples become erect.

6. Take ice cube completely back into mouth. Rub tip of tongue over ice until it becomes cold.

7. Perform cunnilingus.

8. Continue steps 6 and 7 until orgasm or desired consistency of arousal.

The Grapes of Rapture

1 woman, naked
1 man, clothing optional
1 bunch chilled grapes, seedless

1. Have woman stand, legs slightly apart, holding grapes next to vagina.

2. Kneel in front of woman. Kiss and lick ankles, calves, knees and thighs, working your way up.

3. Perform cunnilingus, occasionally removing grape from bunch with teeth and holding it in mouth.

4. Slowly rub clitoris with chilled grape, held between teeth.

5. Use tongue to push grape into vagina. Apply gentle suction to remove. Continue to perform cunnilingus.

6. Repeat steps 3 through 5 until orgasm or desired consistency of arousal.

Kiwi Supreme

1 woman, naked
1 man, clothing optional
1 kiwi fruit, halved

1. Have woman lie on her back.

2. Hold one half of kiwi fruit approximately 4 inches above woman's body and gently squeeze until juice runs over breasts, stomach and thighs.

3. Lick and apply gentle suction to her body, removing juice.

4. Hold other half of kiwi fruit directly over vagina. Gently squeeze until vagina is sufficiently covered in juice.

5. Again, use tongue and gentle suction to remove juice. Begin to perform cunnilingus.

6. Continue until orgasm or desired consistency of arousal.

Penisicle

1 woman, naked
1 man, clothing optional
1 condom, unlubricated

1. Fill condom with water, tie a knot in end and place in freezer for 1 1/2 to 2 hours.

2. Have woman lie on her back.

3. Take condom from freezer and peel sheath from ice.

4. Gently glide condom-shaped icicle over woman's forehead, lips, neck, shoulders, breasts, stomach, thighs and legs.

5. Run icicle around bikini line, then vagina.

6. Delicately touch clitoris with icicle and begin to perform cunnilingus.

7. Continue until orgasm or desired consistency of arousal.

Note: Do not attempt to use condom as a means of contraception after it has been in freezer.

Cotton Can-delight

1 woman, naked
1 man, clothing optional
1 cone cotton candy

1. Have woman lie on her back, eyes closed.

2. Take cotton candy and gently run along length of woman's body.

3. Break off small piece of cotton candy and place on tip of tongue.

4. Press tongue against woman's left nipple, allowing cotton candy to melt.

5. Repeat step 4, this time with right nipple.

6. Place another small piece of cotton candy on tip of tongue and lightly brush against vagina.

7. Press tongue against clitoris, allowing cotton candy to melt.

8. Perform cunnilingus, pausing frequently to repeat steps 6 and 7.

9. Continue until orgasm or desired consistency of arousal.

Bananirvana

1 woman, naked
1 man, clothing optional
1 banana

1. Have woman lie on her back.

2. Peel banana.

3. Center banana against vagina with outermost curved edge resting against the skin.

4. Glide length of banana back and forth along clitoris.

5. Delicately insert tip of banana into vagina.

6. Gradually insert more of banana into vagina, being careful not to insert too much.

7. With part of banana inside vagina, slowly eat exposed portion until lips touch vagina.

8. Perform cunnilingus, applying gentle suction to retrieve remaining portion of banana.

9. Continue until orgasm or desired consistency of arousal.

The Bunny Melt

1 woman, naked
1 man, clothing optional
1 chocolate rabbit, hollow

1. Have woman lie on her back.

2. Glide chocolate rabbit over woman's breasts, stomach, bikini line and legs.

3. Use tips of rabbit ears to gently trace circles around vagina, giving special attention to clitoris.

4. As chocolate begins to soften, delicately insert tips of rabbit ears into vagina and rotate.

5. When chocolate melts, perform cunnilingus.

6. Continue, pausing frequently to reapply chocolate, until orgasm or desired consistency of arousal.

   Note: Chocolate rabbits are generally available in March and April, though they may be frozen for later use.

Showergasm

1 woman, naked
1 man, naked
1 hand-held shower massager

1. Both of you get into shower.

2. Adjust water to desired temperature and activate shower massager.

3. Have woman lie back in tub.

4. Slowly run shower massager over woman's legs, thighs and stomach.

5. With free hand, gently stroke and caress inner thighs and bikini line.

6. Place first and second fingers of free hand on each side of vagina. Gently push skin up and out to help expose clitoris.

7. Run shower massager over clitoris, making sure stream is not so forceful as to cause discomfort or numbness.

8. Continue until orgasm or desired consistency of arousal.

Buzz Lips

1 woman, naked
1 man, clothing optional

1. Have woman lie on her back.

2. Kiss, lick and apply gentle suction to breasts, stomach, legs, thighs and bikini line.

3. Gently spread legs apart, then softly kiss bikini line and vagina.

4. Perform cunnilingus.

5. Gradually shift to a position perpendicular to the woman's body, your head sideways facing vagina.

6. Open mouth slightly and place lips over clitoris. Exhale through mouth and hum.

7. Slowly increase pressure between mouth and clitoris.

8. Continue until orgasm or desired consistency of arousal.

Note: This technique is significantly less awkward when you have music to hum along with.

OrgasM&M

1 woman, naked
1 man, clothing optional
1 piece candy-coated chocolate, green

1. Turn out lights so room is completely dark.

2. Give candy to woman and instruct her to hide it somewhere on her body (she may have to lick the candy beforehand to ensure it remains in place).

3. When candy is hidden, locate it using only your tongue.

4. After candy has been discovered, keep on tip of tongue.

5. Press candy against clitoris and allow to melt.

6. Perform cunnilingus.

7. Continue until orgasm or desired consistency of arousal.

The Venus Butterfly

1 woman, naked
1 man, clothing optional
1 bottle oil

1. Have woman lie on her back.

2. Apply oil to hands and place palm together.

3. Interlock ring fingers of each hand (left ring finger should touch right knuckle, right ring finger should touch left knuckle). All other fingers should remain straight.

4. Insert pinkies into woman's anus.

5. Insert middle fingers into vagina.

6. Place index fingers on both sides of clitoris.

7. Rub hands back and forth, as if trying to warm them.

8. Continue until orgasm or desired consistency of arousal.

Note: If woman is opposed to anal penetration, you may interlock the pinkies as well as the ring fingers.

Sta-puffed Stimulation

1 woman, naked
1 man, clothing optional
1 marshmallow, large

1. Have woman lie on her back.

2. Kiss, lick and apply gentle suction to breasts, stomach, bikini line and thighs.

3. Take marshmallow and slowly roll it over entire length of each vaginal lip.

4. Form a circle with thumb and index finger. Place directly over clitoris.

5. Lick one end of marshmallow and insert between thumb and index finger, moist end down.

6. With other hand, rotate marshmallow back and forth against clitoris, varying speed and intensity.

7. Continue until orgasm or desired consistency of arousal.

The Sensuous Summons

1 woman, naked
1 man, clothing optional
1 bottle oil
1 pillow

1. Have woman lie on her back, pillow under hips.

2. Apply oil to your hands.

3. Caress and gently rub woman's thighs, stomach and bikini line, gradually increasing pressure.

4. Massage area around vagina.

5. Delicately squeeze outer lips of vagina, one at a time, between thumb and index finger. Slowly slide up and down the length of lip.

6. Carefully insert index finger into vagina.

7. With palm facing up, move index finger as if you are summoning a person to come toward you.

8. Use thumb of other hand to gently trace small circles around the clitoris, varying direction and intensity.

9. Continue until orgasm or desired consistency of arousal.

Sue-Bliss

1 woman, naked
1 man, clothing optional
1 jar honey

1. Have woman lie on her left side.

2. Place one drop of honey on right ear lobe, another along hairline behind ear.

3. Trickle honey down right side, from armpit to ankle.

4. Beginning at ear lobe, slowly and methodically lick and apply gentle suction to remove honey from entire right side.

5. When finished, have woman turn over onto right side and repeat steps 2 through 4 on left side.

6. Have woman lie on her back.

7. Place small drops of honey on inner thighs.

8. Remove honey using method described in step 4. With honey still on tongue, perform cunnilingus.

9. Continue until orgasm or desired consistency of arousal.

Strawberry-lation

1 woman, naked
1 man, clothing optional
4 strawberries, sliced
1 can whipped cream

1. Cut strawberries in slices from top to bottom.

2. Have woman lie on her back, legs apart, knees slightly bent.

3. Kiss, lick and apply gentle suction to breasts, stomach, legs, thighs and bikini line.

4. Apply whipped cream liberally around lips of vagina.

5. Take strawberry slices and carefully press them into whipped cream, surrounding vagina.

6. Use tongue to lift strawberries as well as whipped cream into mouth while slowly performing cunnilingus.

7. Continue until orgasm or desired consistency of arousal.

The Tepid Triangle

1 woman, with panties
1 man, clothing optional

1. Have woman sit with legs apart.

2. Take deep breath, open mouth and press against panties, directly over vagina.

3. Exhale warm breath slowly into crotch of panties.

4. Repeat steps 2 and 3 several times.

5. Pull crotch of panties to one side, lick and apply gentle suction to vagina and clitoris.

6. Perform cunnilingus.

7. Continue until orgasm or desired consistency of arousal.

The Sultry Sucker

1 woman, naked
1 man, clothing optional
1 round sucker, any flavor

1. Have woman lie on her back, legs apart, knees slightly bent.

2. Kiss, lick and apply gentle suction to breasts, stomach, legs, thighs and bikini line.

3. Place sucker in mouth.

4. When sufficiently moist, gently rub sucker against lips of vagina.

5. Use mouth to remoisten.

6. Hold sucker in middle of stick with left thumb and index finger. Gently place on clitoris and move in circular motion.

7. Put thumb and index finger of right hand on end of stick. While moving sucker around clitoris with left hand, spin clockwise, then counterclockwise, with right hand, pausing frequently to perform cunnilingus.

8. Continue until orgasm or desired consistency of arousal.

Cake Dec-arousal

1 woman, naked
1 man, clothing optional
1 tube frosting, any color

1. Have woman lie on her back.

2. Apply frosting to breasts, cleavage, stomach and navel. Continue around bikini line, down thighs to knees, then all the way down to feet.

3. Using tongue, delicately remove frosting from woman's body. Alternate between different areas, remembering to lick very slowly.

4. Incorporate gentle flicks of the tongue around vagina and clitoris as you continue to remove frosting.

5. Perform cunnilingus.

6. Continue until orgasm or desired consistency of arousal.

Breath Massage

1 woman, naked
1 man, clothing optional

1. Have woman lie on her stomach.

2. Push hair upward to reveal hairline at back of neck.

3. Place mouth 1/4 to 1/2 inch from neck.

4. Exhale deeply, producing hot breath on hairline.

5. Continue around neck, progressing first toward one ear, then the other.

6. Move down back to buttocks, hovering just above her skin.

7. Slowly move down legs to backs of knees.

8. Have woman roll over on her back.

9. Exhale deeply over inner thighs, moving up to vagina.

10. Perform cunnilingus.

11. Continue until orgasm or desired consistency of arousal.

Egg-stasy

1 woman, naked
1 man, clothing optional
1 egg

1. Boil egg approximately 8 to 10 minutes.

2. Have woman lie on her back.

3. Peel hard-boiled egg, making sure there are no remnants of shell. Egg should be very warm, but not enough to burn.

4. Gently roll egg around woman's stomach.

5. Hold egg with blunt end facing out. Slowly rub nipples and breasts.

6. Turn egg around with pointed end facing out.

7. Glide over and in between lips of vagina.

8. Place egg on clitoris. Use fingers to run circles around clitoris with egg, changing directions frequently.

9. Perform cunnilingus while maintaining stimulation with egg.

10. Continue until orgasm or desired consistency of arousal.

Canta-lucious

1 woman, naked
1 man, clothing optional
1 cantaloupe

1. Cut cantaloupe into equal halves. Remove seeds.

2. Have woman lie on her back.

3. Place cantaloupe halves on woman's breasts. Gently rotate each half in opposite directions.

4. Remove cantaloupe. Using tongue, lick cantaloupe juice from breasts and nipples.

5. Take one cantaloupe half and cut it in half again, producing two quarters.

6. Place one cantaloupe quarter vertically on vagina.

7. Gently rub cantaloupe quarter up and down over vagina.

8. Again, use tongue to lick juice from lips of vagina, gradually beginning to perform cunnilingus.

9. Continue until orgasm or desired consistency of arousal.

Auto-erotica

1 woman, naked
1 man, clothing optional
1 automobile, with sunroof

1. Open sunroof.

2. Have woman climb onto roof and, facing hood, sit with buttocks resting on back edge of sunroof, legs apart, calves resting on windshield.

3. Get into passenger seat on your knees, facing trunk.

4. Position head between woman's legs and perform cunnilingus.

5. Continue until orgasm or desired consistency of arousal.

Note: Before attempting, make sure emergency brake is fully engaged.

C-Delicious

1 woman, naked
1 man, clothing optional
1 compact disc

1. Have woman lie on her back.

2. Place compact disc over woman's right nipple.

3. Use mouth to apply gentle suction, drawing nipple through center hole of compact disc.

4. Repeat step 3 with left nipple.

5. Glide compact disc down woman's stomach to vagina.

6. Place compact disc over clitoris.

7. Use mouth to apply gentle suction to clitoris, drawing it through center hole of compact disc.

8. Rapidly flick tongue over and around clitoris.

9. Continue until orgasm or desired consistency of arousal.

Jell-O-gasm

1 woman, naked
1 man, clothing optional
1 bowl Jell-O, any flavor

1. Have woman lie on her back, legs apart.

2. Place spoonful of Jell-O in your mouth.

3. Push Jell-O to front of mouth, a portion protruding beyond lips.

4. Gently rub Jell-O around inner thighs, bikini line, vagina and clitoris.

5. Use tongue to push Jell-O into vagina. Apply gentle suction to remove.

6. With Jell-O in mouth, perform cunnilingus.

7. Continue until orgasm or desired consistency of arousal.

Entrees
For Both

Notable Potable

1 man, naked
1 woman, naked
2 non-toxic markers, any color

1. Sit on floor facing each other.

2. With marker in hand, man points to woman's breast and asks what she would like done to it.

3. After woman responds, man uses marker to note answer on woman's breast.

4. Woman points to man's inner thigh and asks what he would like done to it.

5. After man responds, woman uses marker to note answer on man's inner thigh.

6. Continue taking turns asking, responding and noting answers on corresponding body parts.

7. When there is no more room to write, climb into bed and make use of your "crib sheets."

8. Shower together afterwards, having one wash off the other's markings.

3-Minute 4-Play

1 man, naked
1 woman, naked
1 egg timer

1. Turn egg timer over. With woman lying on her stomach, man massages shoulders, small of back, buttocks and calves until sand runs out.

2. Repeat step 1 with man.

3. Turn egg timer over. With woman lying on her back, man massages temples, jaw, arms, thighs and gently caresses stomach until sand runs out.

4. Repeat step 3 with man.

5. Turn egg timer over. With woman lying on her back, man kisses, licks and applies gentle suction to nipples, stomach, thighs and genitals until sand runs out.

6. Repeat step 5 with man.

7. Continue to alternate between giving and receiving pleasure in three-minute intervals until orgasm(s) or desired consistency of arousal.

Confection Affection

1 man, naked
1 woman, naked
1 box powdered sugar

1. Woman lies on her back, remaining completely still.

2. Man holds box of powdered sugar 8 to 12 inches above her body, tilts box slightly and taps on bottom. A small portion of powdered sugar should fall onto woman's body.

3. Man continues step 2 until woman's arms, breasts, stomach, bikini line and legs are evenly dusted.

4. Man slowly and deliberately licks powdered sugar from woman's body, gradually moving from least to most sensitive areas.

5. Switch places and repeat from step 1.

    Note: You may want to put powdered sugar into an empty spice bottle with sufficiently sized holes to allow for dusting.

The Twinkling Twosome

1 woman, naked
1 man, naked
4 strings Christmas lights
1 extension cord

1. Stand facing each other.

2. Man connects two strings of lights and, beginning at ankles, carefully wraps lights around woman's left leg, waist, stomach, chest, shoulder and left arm.

3. Woman connects two strings of lights and, beginning at ankles, carefully wraps lights around man's left leg, waist, stomach, chest, shoulder and left arm.

4. Plug strings into extension cord and plug into wall outlet.

5. Turn out all other lights.

6. Begin foreplay, then intercourse, with lights blinking or static, being careful not to lie on or crush bulbs.

> Note: Check all strings and extension cord beforehand for frayed wiring or damaged bulbs.

The Vineyard's Mist

1 man, naked
1 woman, naked
1 bottle wine
1 spray bottle, clean

1. Fill spray bottle with wine. Adjust nozzle so it gives fine mist.

2. Take turns spraying mist over partner's face, neck, shoulders, chest, back, legs and genitals.

3. Slowly lick and apply gentle suction to partner's body, removing wine from skin.

4. Gradually advance to mutual oral sex and/or intercourse.

Note: Make sure spray bottle is completely clean. New bottle is recommended. Do not use bottle that has ever contained anything toxic, such as cleaning or gardening products.

Carnal Coupons

1 man
1 woman
1 pad notepaper

1. Make a mental list of your partner's five favorite sexual pleasures.

2. On separate pieces of paper, draw coupons that entitle your partner to all five treats, redeemable at any time.

3. Present them to your partner as a birthday or anniversary gift, or simply as a surprise.

Chocolate Cherries Jubilee

1 woman, naked
1 man, naked
1 chocolate-covered cherry

1. Man takes chocolate-covered cherry, turns it upside-down and bites off bottom (flat) portion.

2. He then bites bottom portion into equal halves and rests them on woman's nipples.

3. Using finger to hold cherry inside chocolate cup, he slowly pours cherry liquid over woman's thighs.

4. Using tongue and gentle suction, man removes liquid from woman's body and melted chocolate from nipples.

5. Setting aside chocolate cup, man inserts cherry into mouth, performs cunnilingus, pushes cherry into vagina with tongue and applies gentle suction to remove. He then swallows cherry and continues until orgasm or desired consistency of arousal.

6. Woman takes hollow chocolate cup and, with man lying on his back, places on top of erect penis and performs fellatio.

7. She then continues until orgasm or desired consistency of arousal.

Erotic Roulette

1 woman
1 man
1 jar, empty
1 note pad, small

1. Whenever one of you comes up with something new you would like to try in bed (or wherever), write it on pad, fold paper and place in jar. Always use the same pad so all entries look identical in jar.

2. Keep jar in nightstand or other convenient, but inconspicuous, location.

3. Before making love, select one piece of paper from jar and, if both are willing, incorporate request into session.

4. Alternate between granting one of your partner's requests, then your own.

Nipple Shot

1 woman, topless
1 man, topless
1 shaker salt
1 lemon, quartered
1 bottle tequila

1. Woman lies on her back.

2. Man licks woman's left nipple and applies salt.

3. He then rubs lemon quarter over right nipple, gently squeezing lemon to extract juice.

4. Finally, he fills woman's navel up with tequila.

5. With a flat, open tongue, man quickly licks the salt off left nipple, sucks tequila from navel and swallows, then gently sucks lemon juice from right nipple.

6. Switch places and repeat steps 1 through 5 using man's nipples and navel.

Note: If partner's navel is an "outie," you may substitute with shot glass.

Fore-Playback

1 woman, naked
1 man, naked
1 tape recorder, with headphones

1. Take tape recorder into a room by yourself.

2. For fifteen minutes, visualize everything you would like your partner to do to give you the perfect foreplay experience.

3. As you see the image in your mind, describe exactly what your partner is doing into tape recorder. Speak slowly and in as much detail as possible.

4. At the end of fifteen minutes, turn recorder off and give it to your partner.

5. Have your partner repeat steps 1 through 3.

6. Rewind tape to the beginning. With headphones on, so only they can hear, have your partner listen to the tape and act out exactly what you described.

7. When partner's voice appears on tape, reverse roles.

Pudding Pleasure

1 man, naked
1 woman, naked
1 bowl pudding, any flavor
1 blanket

1. Sit on blanket facing each other, bowl of pudding between you.

2. Take turns dipping first and second fingers into bowl, scooping out generous servings of pudding and spreading liberally over partner's chest, stomach, genitals, legs and any other areas you or your partner desires.

3. Move bowl off blanket.

4. Each of you lie on your side, your head at partner's feet.

5. Simultaneously use tongues and mouths to kiss, lick and suck pudding from each other's body, eventually performing oral sex.

6. Continue until orgasm(s) or desired consistency of arousal.

Pasta Passion

1 man, naked
1 woman, naked
2 lasagna noodles

1. Boil lasagna noodles for approximately 8 to 10 minutes. Remove one noodle and allow to cool.

2. Woman lies on her back.

3. Man rubs lasagna noodle over woman's stomach, making sure it not too hot.

4. He then lays noodle over vagina and gently rubs up and down, eventually performing cunnilingus.

5. Continue until orgasm or desired consistency of arousal.

6. Woman removes other lasagna noodle from pot and has man lie on his back.

7. She rubs noodle over man's stomach, making sure it is not too hot.

8. Women then wraps noodle around penis and uses hand to stimulate manually, eventually performing fellatio.

9. Continue until orgasm or desired consistency of arousal.

69 Card Pick-Up

1 woman, naked
1 man, naked

1. Man lies face up on bed, legs bent over edge, feet touching floor.

2. Woman positions herself on all fours over man, vagina even with his face, her face even with penis.

3. Use mouths and tongues to stimulate each other simultaneously.

4. Man places arms securely around woman's waist.

5. Man slides buttocks to edge of bed and carefully sits up. Woman now rests upper legs on man's shoulders.

6. Man carefully rises from bed and stands. Woman is now upside-down.

7. Continue using mouths and tongues to stimulate each other until orgasm(s) or desired consistency of arousal.

> Note: Use extreme caution throughout. Do not attempt if under the influence of alcohol or any other controlled substance.

Desserts

Country Coitus

1 woman, naked
1 man, naked
1 porch swing, adjustable

1. Adjust porch swing chains to proper height for intercourse.

2. Woman sits in porch swing, legs apart, vagina even with edge of seat.

3. Man, standing or kneeling, inserts penis into vagina.

4. Woman raises legs and places them on man's shoulders.

5. Man uses hands to grasp seat of swing and rocks it back and forth.

6. Continue until orgasm(s) or desired consistency of arousal.

In-line Enchantment

1 man, naked
1 woman, naked
1 pair in-line skates

1. Woman puts on skates and stands on smooth surface, such as kitchen floor.

2. From behind, man inserts penis into vagina and places hands around woman's waist.

3. Man guides woman around room, using forward thrusts to facilitate motion.

4. Continue until orgasm(s) or desired consistency of arousal.

Note: You can substitute roller skates for the in-lines.

Patio-gasm

1 **woman, naked**
1 **man, naked**
1 **lounge chair, webbed**
2 **pillows**
1 **roll masking tape**

1. Adjust back of lounge chair to upright position.

2. Place pillows lengthwise directly underneath lounge chair.

3. Pull center-most webbing apart and tape to other straps, creating an opening in center of chair at least 5 inches wide.

4. Woman sits in lounge chair, vagina positioned above opening.

5. Man lies underneath lounge chair, using pillows under back and buttocks to bring him to suitable height.

6. Man inserts penis into vagina and thrusts hips upward.

7. Continue until orgasm(s) or desired consistency of arousal.

Hy-stair-ia

1 man, naked
1 woman, naked
1 staircase

1. Woman sits on second stair from bottom, legs apart.

2. Man kneels on first stair from bottom and inserts penis into vagina.

3. During intercourse, woman wraps legs around man. Man wraps arms around woman's torso.

4. Man straightens knees and lifts woman to next stair.

5. Repeat steps 3 and 4 until woman reaches top of staircase.

6. Continue until orgasm(s) or desired consistency of arousal.

The Horizontal Tune-Up

1 woman, naked
1 man, naked
1 automotive creeper

1. Woman lies face down on creeper, legs apart.

2. Man kneels behind woman, assumes push-up-like position and inserts penis into vagina.

3. Woman uses arms to push against floor, moving creeper backwards.

4. Man thrusts hips to push creeper forward.

5. Continue until orgasm(s) or desired consistency of arousal.

Note: The "creeper" is a skateboard-like device mechanics use to roll under a car. They are available at most automotive and discount stores.

The Titillating Table

1 woman, naked
1 man, naked
1 dining table

1. Woman lies face up on table, buttocks on edge, legs apart.

2. Man, standing in front of woman, inserts penis into vagina.

3. Woman brings legs up to chest and extends, resting heels or calves on man's shoulders.

4. Continue until orgasm(s) or desired consistency of arousal.

Horn of Panty

1 man, clothed
1 woman, clothed
1 old pair panties

1. Without man knowing, woman cuts hole in crotch of panties, no larger than necessary for penis to fit through.

2. She then puts on panties and outerwear.

3. Woman initiates foreplay (see *Entrees*), undressing man.

4. Woman has man undress her, except for panties.

5. Select a mutually desirable position and begin intercourse.

6. Continue until orgasm(s) or desired consistency of arousal.

Waterbedlum

1 woman, naked
1 man, naked
1 bottle baby oil
1 waterbed, no sheets

1. Man and woman sit on waterbed facing each other.

2. Apply baby oil liberally to each other's arms, legs, backs, stomachs and any other areas you wish.

3. Touch, rub and fondle each other to heighten the effect of baby oil. Gradually move on to intercourse.

4. Continue until orgasm(s) or desired consistency of arousal.

Gotta Have Mower

1 man, naked except for footwear
1 woman, naked except for footwear
1 riding lawn mower

1. Man sits in lawn mower seat and, making sure it is in neutral and blades are fully disengaged, starts mower.

2. Woman places feet on running boards, straddles man's lap, grasps penis and inserts into vagina.

3. Woman flexes knees to provide up and down motion while man throttles lawn mower to vary intensity of vibration.

4. Continue until orgasm(s) or desired consistency of arousal.

> Note: Use extreme caution throughout. Do not attempt without protective footwear. Do not attempt when mower blades are engaged. Do not attempt if either party is under the influence of alcohol or any other controlled substance.